Comforting Mandalas
Grief Healing

Written & Illustrated by
Anne Manera

Book design & Cover art
By Anne Manera

ISBN: 1544751443
ISBN-13: 978-1544751443

Follow Anne Manera

Website / Blog –
www.annemanera.com

Facebook –
www.facebook.com/annemanerascoloringbooks

Facebook Coloring Group-
www.facebook.com/groups/coloralongwithannemanera/

Facebook COLOR-ALONG Coloring Group –
www.facebook.com/groups/JustColorGroup

Twitter –
www.twitter.com/annemanera

Instagram –
www.instagram.com/anne.manera

Cherished memories held close to my heart

A feather

drifted

near me,

I know

it was you

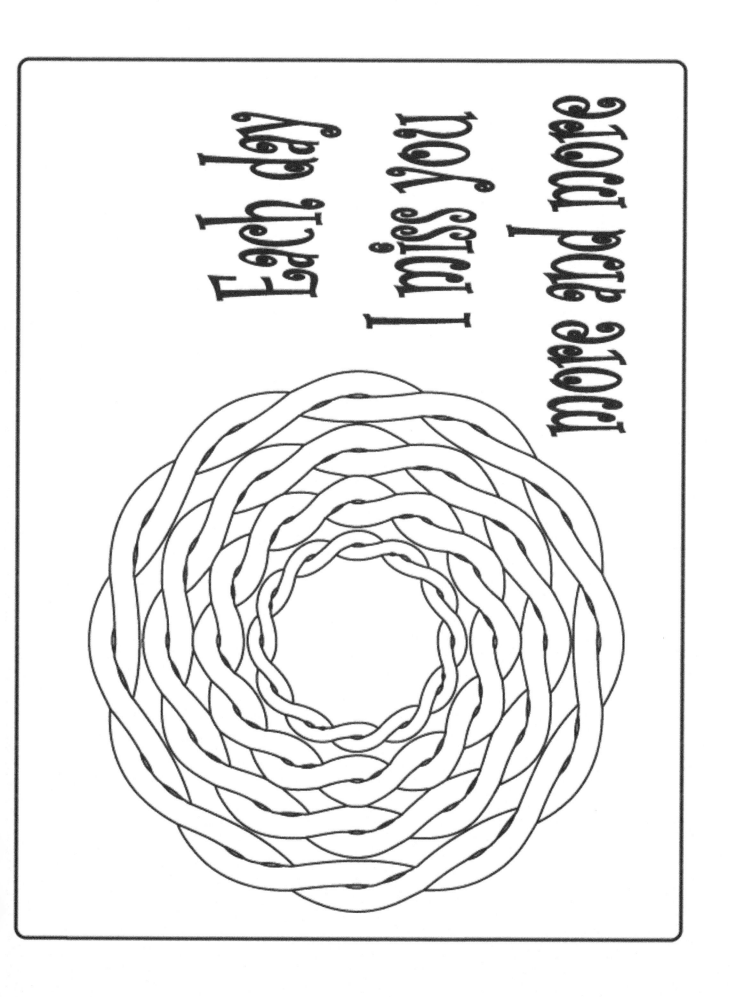

Each day
I miss you
more and more

Two souls holding hands

An Angel walks beside me

Our hearts still beat as one

I am
learning
to live
without
you

Blowing
you a
kiss in
heaven

Treasured memories written on my heart

When you
left, all
the colors
left my
world

I wish
heaven had
a phone,
so I could
talk to you
one more time

Another day without you...

I never knew I could love so deeply

I miss the person you believed me to be

I tell
myself
I am
stronger
than
I think

I never want to forget how your voice sounds

I never
knew how
much
sorrow
my heart
could hold

I had
so many
dreams
about
you and me

Sometimes you just need to let the tears out

It's okay to not be okay

Everytime
I pause,
I think
of you

Cherished memories held close to my heart

A feather
drifted
near me,
I know
it was you

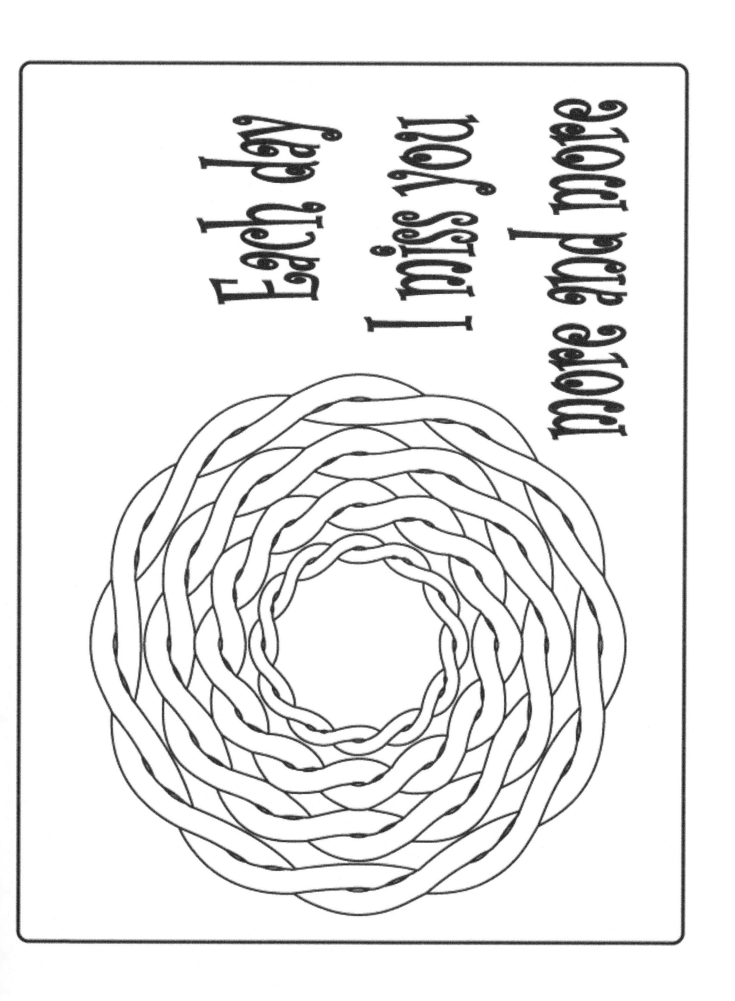

Each day
I miss you
more and more

Today
was a
good day!

An
Angel
walks
beside me

I am
learning
to live
without
you

Blowing
you a
kiss in
heaven

Treasured memories written on my heart

When you
left, all
the colors
left my
world

I wish
heaven had
a phone,
so I could
talk to you
one more time

Another day without you...

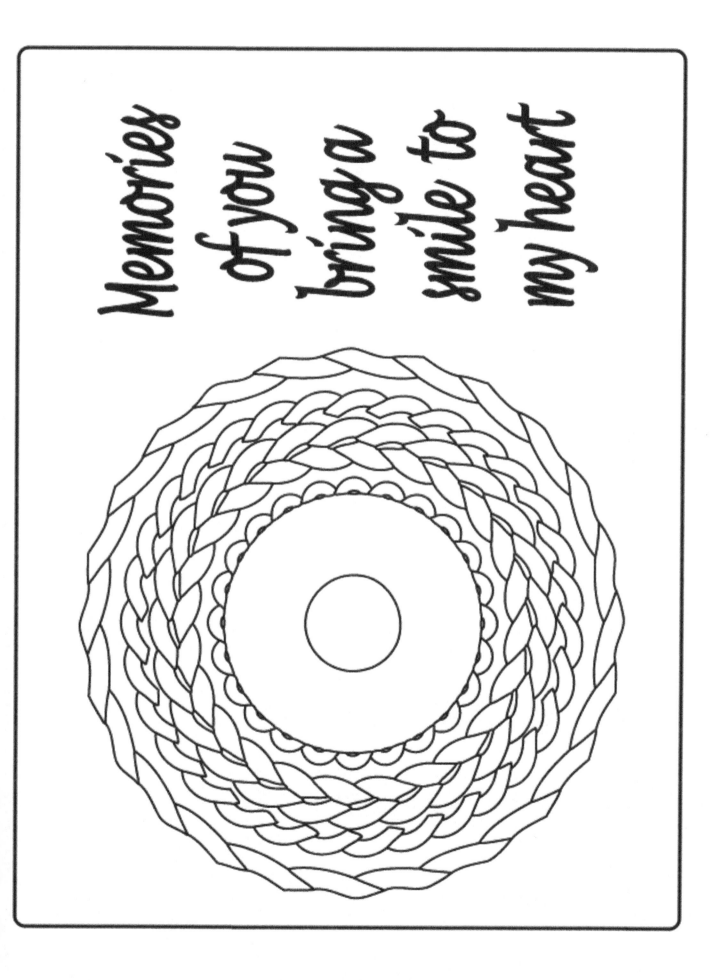

Memories of you bring a smile to my heart

I never
knew I
could
love
so deeply

I miss the person you believed me to be

I tell myself I am stronger than I think

I never want to forget how your voice sounds

I never
knew how
much
sorrow
my heart
could hold

I had

so many

dreams

about

you and me

Sometimes you just need to let the tears out

It's okay to not be okay

Made in the USA
Coppell, TX
21 December 2021

69780656R00059